EVIL MONEY
EVIL CREDIT

Carol,

Best wishes on your political future.

Sincerely,

[illegible signature]

9/17/09

EVIL MONEY
EVIL CREDIT

Alton J. Jones

HIGH TOWER BOOKS™

Phoenix, Arizona

First Edition

ISBN 0-9774601-0-X

Editing by Robin Gentry
Cover design by Corine Kirschbaum

Printed and bound in the United States of America

HIGH TOWER BOOKS™

2425 East Camelback Road
Suite 950
Phoenix, Arizona 85016
Sales@HighTowerBooks.com
(888) 308-5858

www.HighTowerBooks.com

Table of Contents

Dedication

For the family, friends, collection agencies, financial institutions, credit bureaus and firsthand experience... all of which helped inspire me to write this book.

Special thanks to Robin Gentry for all of her editorial assistance, Corine Kirschbaum for her graphic contribution, and George Rosenthal and all the staff at the Insurance Information Institute.

Introduction

It seems to remain common that many consumers would rather buy now and deal with the consequences later. They deny the pending outcome of their overextension. Their misguided belief is that as long as they do not think about the outcome, it will mysteriously go away. If only they could win the lottery, be rear-ended by someone with a luxury car, or accidentally slip on a puddle of water in a major department store and sue for store negligence in an effort to collect a large settlement.

You may be familiar with the phrase, "Money is the root of all evil." This phrase appears to imply that having credit is evil or that being financially successful is a direct result of doing something evil. If you continue to believe credit and money is the root of all evil and therefore something to be avoided and ignored, you may continue to be reluctant to take the necessary steps to enhance your credit performance.

As a result of not taking the necessary steps and ignoring your credit report, you may inadvertently victimize yourself and end up paying higher interest charges, loan fees, and even insurance premiums. You <u>can</u> be in the power seat in negotiations. You <u>can</u> receive approvals faster and easier than ever before.

Note from the Author

I have written this book to be easy to read and understandable, with a special section called "My Advice." It is a conversation, personally, between myself and my reader(s). You may want to utilize the "Notes" section to document your thoughts, feelings, and list the people you wish to either contact for your new credit project – or even friends with which you may want to share this information.

This information was garnered from personal experience and dedication to improving my life. It is my hope that it will assist you in avoiding as many unpleasant experiences as possible, while also providing a clear path toward your financial and emotional health – as they often travel hand-in-hand.

I want to hear from you. My e-mail address is AltonJJones@HighTowerBooks.com. Please use it to ask questions or make comments on how the book affected you, or suggestions on how it can be improved.

Forward

This book explores the basics of credit and financial accountability, along with the necessity for establishing, maintaining, and/or repairing personal credit.

This book was written for you, if you are between the ages 18-40 and have:

- Been told you have very poor credit
- Been told you have poor credit
- Been told you have fair credit
- Been denied credit
- Been told your credit score is 630 or lower from Experian, Equifax or TransUnion
- Rented an apartment
- Rented furniture
- Utilized the service of a payday lending facility

The Basics

What is Credit?

Credit is considered the ability to borrow or to purchase goods and services with payment delayed beyond delivery based on your payment history and reputation.

By having a good credit reputation for repaying your debt on time, the more willing a lender will be to extend you credit. Creditors confirm your history of how timely you have paid debts in the past by generating a credit check. To determine if the chances of the consumer will pay the debt timely, most lenders use some type of scoring system.

A variety of factors are involved in the overall mathematical scoring, such as how many times during a certain period the consumer has applied for new credit and how timely payments were made in the past.

One of the other continuing beliefs among consumers is that financial freedom comes from paying off all bills and being debt free. As a result of this belief, lenders will take your payments, but your record of timely payment of debts will stop.

In the case of paying off debts in lump sum payments; the consumer has paid the debt in full; however, the continuing history of timely payments which is actually needed to establish new credit has stopped. Believe it or not, NOT having a continual credit history can make obtaining new credit as difficult as if one had credit problems.

Notes:

What Information is in My Credit Report?

There are a variety of items referenced on credit reports, such as your name, aliases, current and previous addresses, social security number, spouse's name, current and previous employers, past and present credit accounts. Public information such as bankruptcy records, state and county court records of tax liens and monetary judgments are also listed.

The three main credit bureaus, Equifax, Experian and TransUnion, have different formats and procedures to display consumer information for each account, such as your credit limits, previous and current loan amounts, balances, and payment patterns. All of this information comes from companies the consumer has done business with in the past.

The report will also reference the business names of those companies who have obtained a copy of the consumer's credit report.

If the consumer has filed any disputes against the information referenced on their credit report, it will also be referenced, as well as the status if the investigation.

Notes:

How Often Should My Credit Report and Credit Score be Checked?

Knowing your credit score, which credit bureau the creditor uses (Experian, Equifax or TransUnion), and the minimum score needed to extend credit to you will save you from further damaging your credit by generating an unnecessary inquiry, which actually deducts points from your credit score.

For example, if you visit a car audio retailer and the minimum credit score needed for approval of "90 Days Same As Cash" financing was 650, and it uses Equifax to obtain scoring, it will be of no use to have a score of 655 with Experian if your Equifax score was 648. Each bureau is its own entity and keeps its own records.

My Advice: If you are diligently monitoring the completion of your credit repair and increase of score, I would recommend every 30 days from the initial dispute letter sent to one or all credit bureaus. Otherwise, check every six months.

Notes:

What is a Credit Score?

Your credit score, often referred to as a FICO, PLUS or Fair Isaac score, is a numerical score on you, the consumer, and your credit worthiness/risk on whether you will pay back a loan in a timely manner. The numeric ranges, depending on the credit bureau, are from the low 300s to mid 850s with Equifax, mid 300s to low 820s with Experian, and low 400s to low 900s with TransUnion. The ranges are also generalized as Very Poor, Poor, Fair, Good and Excellent/Very Good.

A score of about 638 with each bureau would probably place you in the "Fair" category. It is my opinion that obtaining a credit score in the mid-700s would enable you to be in a strategic position in getting significantly lower interest rates. Obtaining a score in the coveted 800s will enable you to be in a more commanding position for rates such as 0%.

Whether the lender uses a score from one bureau or an algorithm of the three, they all have one purpose: To summarize your credit worthiness and make that information available to future inquiries.

Please keep in mind that your score is just one factor used in processing an application. Lenders may also consider other factors, such as one's annual income and length of employment, when you apply for a loan.

My Advice: Is it in the lending institution's best interest that you have a high score? Not necessarily. There are a couple of theories regarding credit scores and how lending institutions may profit from your score. Rest assured, their number one goal is profit – most of the time at your expense.

For example, the lower your credit score, the greater your risk factor and rationale for charging you higher interest rates. On the other side of coin, the higher your credit score, the lower your risk factor and rationale for charging lower interest rates on a higher loan amount.

Notes:

How Do I Get a Copy of My Credit Report and Score?

The three bureaus, Equifax, Experian, and TransUnion, can be contacted via telephone or online at:

- **www.Equifax.com**
- **www.Experian.com**
- **www.TransUnion.com**

Each site has a link near the top of its home page for personal or business services. Click the link referencing "Personal" to begin the online ordering process of your personal credit report and score.

My Advice: Save yourself the time and headache and order your credit report online. Local libraries often have free online access. If you encounter a problem with ordering online, make the telephone call, or mail your request along with your personal check and request form.

It is best to order credit reports from each separate bureau, rather than obtain a multi-bureau credit report from a report consolidation service. If you decide to submit a dispute, you are going to need a separate confirmation number as a reference, which are obtained by ordering separate reports.

Remember, there are thousands of disputes processed by these bureaus each day. Any missing outdated or inaccurate data you provide may delay the completion of your dispute's resolution.

Notes:

Credit Report Inquiries

Every time you apply for a credit card or complete any credit application, your report is negatively affected and a "Hard Inquiry" is generated. Hard inquiries lower scores. The more hard inquiries generated, the lower the score and the higher your perceived risk factor. Thus, the perceived justification for higher interest rates for consumers with low credit scores.

A "Soft Inquiry" is an inquiry which does not negatively affect your score nor add an inquiry to your report. Companies interested in determining whether you are an attractive customer for product or service solicitation will often generate this type of inquiry. Employers may often use this type of inquiry to determine whether or not to hire you. Remember, it is a determination of potential risk.

Receiving numerous "Pre-Approved" credit card applications can be tempting to accept. Your contact information has been shared. Do you read the "small print" text on the information/product request and credit related applications you submit? Most likely not. Now, promise yourself you'll never submit another request without taking a few minutes to read the terms of your agreement with the creditor. You may be agreeing to the sharing of your contact information – or other terms that you may not want.

My Advice: Stop further mail solicitations by "opting out." (See Opting Out in the next section.)

Notes:

Opting Out

American consumer mailboxes are bombarded with tempting offers of credit or merchandise, such as catalogs, vacations, or credit cards. However, while many welcome these solicitations, others do not.

If you want your name and address removed from mailing lists obtained from the main consumer credit reporting agencies visit:

www.Optoutprescreen.com

To be removed from mailing and telephone lists contact:

Direct Marketing Association
Mail Preference Service
P.O. Box 643
Carmel, New York 10512

Include with your request:

- First, middle, and last names (including Jr., Sr., III)
- Current address
- Home area code and telephone number (only for Telephone Preference Service)

Ordering Your Report on the Phone

Visit each bureau's Website and find the correct telephone number to call, as their telephone numbers may have changed by the time this book is published. If necessary, find a creative way to get online access to obtain the telephone numbers.

My Advice: It is my opinion to use a land-based phone line to call and inquire about any information regarding your credit. In using a cellular phone, it has been my experience that signals seem to mysteriously disconnect at the most inopportune times.

If you are successful in reaching a customer service representative or become connected to an automated system, be prepared by having either your credit or debit card in hand. The automated systems appear to have response time clocks and may disconnect your call if your response is delayed too long.

Notes:

What if You Find a Reporting Error?

By now, you should have gone through the steps to obtain and carefully review all three individually ordered credit reports. If you find an error, you may dispute it online for the fastest response. Typically, after a dispute is generated online, you should receive a printed response within a week. Generally, each bureau will respond to you within 30 calendar days of your online dispute submittal and may send you incremental changes during that period. Add seven calendar days if you mailed your dispute.

A credit/debit card is required to order reports and scores online. Personal checks are accepted with mailed requests. If you are concerned about using your credit/debit card online, you can call each bureau with the phone number referenced on its site. Your call will be answered electronically, placed in a queue where you are often forced to listen to advertisements and navigate through its automated call system until you speak to a customer service representative.

My Advice: Be specific by including the auto-generated confirmation/reference number from the report you purchased, creditor account number(s) of an item you feel is in error, and explain exactly why you feel it is inaccurate. Attaching copies of relevant supporting documentation would be helpful. General statements about inaccuracies often do not provide enough detail to help effectively resolve disputes.

Notes:

Can Credit Repair Clinics Fix My Bad Credit?

Consumers pay hundreds of dollars to pay so-called "credit clinics" to fix their credit reports. If you are reading this book, then you have made an additional step towards further effectively managing your credit and personal finance.

My Advice: Do it yourself!

Notes:

How Long Does Information Remain Stored on Your Credit Report?

Missed payments and most public record items remain on the credit report for about seven years, with the exception of Chapters 7, 11 and 12 bankruptcies, which remain for about 10 years, as well as unpaid tax liens, which remain for about 15 years.

Active positive information may remain on the report indefinitely.

Requests for your credit history remain on the credit report for about to two years.

Some credit bureaus reference in the "Remarks" section of a negative posting, the estimated month and year, which the negative posting will be removed.

Notes:

Do Credit Scores Affect My Insurance?

Insurance is one of the unavoidable necessities in life. In most states, it is even the law. The Insurance Information Institute (2005), an organization that formed to improve public understanding of insurance, states:

> *An insurance score is a numerical ranking based on a person's credit history. Actuarial studies show that how a person manages his or her financial affairs, which is what an insurance score indicates, is a good predictor of insurance claims. Insurance scores are used to help insurers differentiate between lower and higher insurance risks and thus charge a premium equal to the risk they are assuming. Statistically, people who have a poor insurance score are more likely to file a claim.*

Hartwig and Wilkinson (2003) stated in their studies for the Insurance Information Institute "...a [Washington State study] ...revealed a strong link between credit standing and crash frequency. According to this analysis, some 64 percent of drivers with zero crashes had good credit, while just 35 percent had bad credit." (p. 5)

Visit **www.Choicetrust.com**. This Website provides information about the C.L.U.E.® Personal Property report, which contains a five-year history of losses, associated with an individual and his/her personal property.

Notes:

Collection Agency Report Listings

After a designated period of waiting to receive your past due balance, your debt may either be sold to a collection agency at a discounted rate or transferred to the creditor's collection department. In each case, the apparent object is to collect as much of the original past due total as possible using more aggressive tactics. Each time your account is sold or an agency was bought by a rival firm, a new account number is often created. This further complicates the tracking and identifying of the original account number.

You will also note on your credit report that the complete account numbers are disguised with leading or trailing letters and/or numbers for security.

My Advice: It has been my experience to call the originating creditors and collection agencies to identify and document the complete account number(s) for your records

Notes:

Within Range

Accomplishing Your Credit Goals

Having improved credit can make a significant impact on a person's life.

Imagine the respect you will receive as you walk into a car dealership, acknowledge the car you want and that your credit score is over 800. Of course, you insist on the lowest interest rate available.

Can it happen to you? Yes. It can. It is possible for you to get the coveted over 800 range. If you use the following suggestions, you are well on your way to getting your highest score ever.

My Advice: Keep credit accounts for more than five years. It is like having a friend you have known for years. When your credit is evaluated (searching for a new friend), a snapshot is taken of how well you have treated your old friend. If you have abused your old friend and not paid him on time, why would a new friend (creditor) want to be associated with you? Even if you seldom use the card, pay it on time.

1. **Delete various entries of your name** on the credit report and reference only your full legal name. If your full legal name is John Samuel Doe and your credit report reference John Samuel Doe and state that your alias(es) are John S. Doe and J.S. Doe, send each bureau a letter referencing the incorrect rendering of your name. I have provided sample letters to assist you in writing them.

2. **Delete incorrect addresses referenced on your credit report** and update the bureau with your present address. If you have a post office box as a primary address, you may want to consider obtaining some sort of physical address.

3. **Order a free copy of your credit report at least once a year** from one of the three bureaus. Put a note in your calendar as a reminder to do so. The free report will not come with your credit score. TransUnion may still provide the ability to purchase your score separately, for a fee, by calling (866) 726-7388. Check the free credit report you receive to see if that bureau references the availability of this option.

4. **Order a copy of your report and score every six months** from each separate bureau. Spend the money. It's worth it... you're worth it!

5. **Pay off debts such as high interest rate credit cards and high interest rate loans** from finance companies in lump sums, if possible. Student loans, which provide student loan interest tax advantages can be paid incrementally to maintain a continual credit history of prompt payment.

6. **Visit www.CreditCardRatings.com to learn what consumers say** about obtaining higher credit card limits and which credit card providers are more beneficial to you.

7. **Have a balance of no more than 30% on your credit card account** and pay it on time.

8. **Shop for mortgage loans within a two-week period or less of your first inquiry.** Do your mortgage shopping online for a lower interest rate to reduce the potential overhead cost you may incur by using the traditional lending method.

9. **Never be late in paying your mortgage.**

10. **Do not inquire for credit shortly before applying for a home loan.** Wait until after your loan is approved and processed before applying for credit on items such as appliances, cars, and/or home furnishings.

11. **Open a checking account with direct deposit and use the issued debit card** to make and track daily purchases. This is a good exercise in financial discipline.

12. **Purchase financial tracking software,** such as Microsoft Money® or Intuit QuickBooks®. Download your bank statements daily if you have an Internet connection. This is a great exercise in financial discipline.

13. **Have some type of calendar system to remind you of due dates** and designate each paycheck to cover the bills, which can be timely paid within that period. You will notice that there are months where you are paid three times within that month. Diligently maintaining your bi-weekly bill payments will save you money in interest rates for early bill payments within the creditor's payment cycle.

14. **If you have more than three credit cards, pay off and close the most recently acquired account(s).** If you use the remaining cards infrequently, store them in a secure place. Use those accounts occasionally, at least once every three months, for small purchases. This will inform the creditor that you are still interested in maintaining your credit account with them. It is advisable to pay off infrequently used accounts and keep them open. Remember, account longevity plays an important role in your credit score.

15. **Be cautious of balance transfer offers.** Remember, each time you submit an application for that new card a hard inquiry will be generated.

16. **Do not let your account become late.** If you believe this in unavoidable, do not let it be more that 29 days late. Creditors often report on a 30, 60, 90 and 120 system.

17. **Vehicle repossession has a negative impact on your credit.** This also applies to voluntary repossession.

18. **Read about and weigh all the positive and negative outcomes before filing bankruptcy.** You may decide that it is your only option. You may decide to tighten your budget even more and work your way through it by speaking directly with the creditors/collection agencies. It is my opinion that it is better to be honest with the creditors, own up to your financial irresponsibility and work through it.

Avoiding calls and letters is a sure way to dig further into a financial hole. If it boils down to selling your home for less than what you believe it is worth, but above market value, so be it.

19. **Consider the advantages and disadvantages of credit counseling services.** With time and persistence, you can do what the counseling services offer. You may have to pay them a fee of some sort to get the creditor to lower your balance. The amount you are paying to the counseling service might be slightly lower than what you would have paid directly to the creditor.

    The creditor probably reduced the interest rate charged to you in an effort to collect a portion of the balance with the assistance of the counseling service. All the while, you could be paying lower payments to a counseling service which may or may not pay on time. You will subsequently be marked as late.

20. **Remove consumer statements from all of your credit bureau reports.** For example, statements explaining your divorce and loss of employment. Having this information readily available may give lenders one more reason to question your risk factor.

21. **Consider the disadvantages of your credit being tarnished if you co-sign on a loan** and the primary account holder makes a late payment.

22. **Consider the disadvantages of your credit being tarnished if you decide to lend your credit cards to friends** and your credit limit is exceeded.

23. **If you have collection accounts, call the collection agency and ask for a letter referencing the agreed settlement amount to be faxed to you.**

If you have a computer with an Internet connection and an email address, but not a fax machine, I would recommend free electronic faxing services such as jConnect Free™ provided by J2 Global Communications. Visit **www.J2.com**, or call toll-free (888) 718-2000. This service converts incoming faxes into email capable, viewable and printable attachments. You can obtain a free fax number and have the attachment sent to your personal email address. The free fax number assigned to you may not be in your own area code. You can use up to 20 fax pages per month. If you exceed this limit, you will receive an email advising that you risk losing your account. So use this service sparingly.

Ask the collection agency if they accept Western® Union Quick Collect®, payments. Do not send money orders for payoff. A money order only leaves you with a stub referencing that you purchased it. Unfortunately, it does not provide a means of tangible proof of payment to the agency, as you would receive with a Western Union® transaction or bank returnable personal or bank check.

If the agency accepts Western Union® payments, obtain its Code City and Code State and go to a facility near you to send your payment. You will receive a Money Transfer Control Number (MTCN) confirming the transaction. Call the collection agency to provide a status update and provide the MTCN number. Then mail copies of the agreement letter and MTCN receipt to each credit bureau and request an update to your file.

There are two common consumer behaviors of resolving a collection account posting on a credit report. One is to pay the debt; the other is to ignore the debt and let the credit bureau remove it once it passes the end of the reportable period, which is approximately seven years. *(I paid my debts and accepted the consequences of knowing it would further delay the removal of my negative credit history.)*

24. **If you have to take a second or third job to pay off your debt, do it.**

25. **Discuss and reveal your credit history and/or score to your potential spouse.** If your loved one is financially irresponsible, what other areas in their lives are they irresponsible with? Many marriages are doomed for failure long before the wedding day, because of the lack of disclosure.

    Imagine you got married to whom you perceived as Mr. or Ms. Right. A baby is born and a home is needed. In the purchasing process, your spouse's poor credit makes buying the home difficult.

    Would you be willing to add additional stress to the marriage by asking your spouse to sign a waiver form so that the one with the better credit can purchase the home solely in his or her name?

26. **Start saving!** Have enough of a financial safety net to support yourself in case of an emergency.

27. **Be cautious of signing personal guarantees when applying for corporate credit accounts.** Corporate accounts may appear on your personal credit report. If you sign a "personal guarantee" in an agreement, your personal credit profile may be jeopardized if your business experiences financial difficulties.

28. **Avoid finance charges.** Pay the new balance due on the due date each month, as reflected on each monthly statement to avoid finance charges for that billing period. The total balance due on that card may be higher, but the remaining amount due applies to the next billing period and can be paid the following month.

Correspondence

Maintaining supporting documentation can be tedious, but well worth the time and effort involved. Document everything!

My Advice: Make front and back copies of any proof of payoff, letters, emails, and screen copies of online forms you submit and keep them until the end of the posting's reportable period. Some bureaus may provide the option for users to generate a printable version, before submittal, of their online dispute response. Some may not. Therefore, make and print your own screen copy of the response you are about to submit until you confirm the availability of the screen copy option provided by the bureau.

Scanning a supporting document and saving it onto a CD or a computer's hard drive as a .tif file, will extend the longevity of its life. Ink fades over time and paper can be easily misplaced or damaged.

With each new report version received, review it, transfer any old notes from the previous version, write any new notes of any bureau changes made on the latest version and discard the old one.

You may discover that a new collection agency purchased an account and created a new account number for this file. Making any applicable notes on the latest report version you receive, will assist you in monitoring the posting's progress until it reaches the end of the reportable period.

When my detailed dispute explanation required more text space than what was made available online, I submitted a brief explanation and also mailed a more detailed letter similar to those provided below. Ensure that each credit bureau's letter contains the reference number you received upon purchase of your credit report.

General Improvement

Date

Your Address

Creditor
Address
City, State Zip Code

ATTN: Contact person name, if known

RE: Credit Report - (Creditor name)
Account Number (Insert account number)

Dear (Contact person name):

I am in the process of cleaning up my credit report to improve my scores and request your assistance. I initially opened an account on or around (Date) under account number 123456789. Since then, I have refinanced this loan and new account numbers are referenced on my report.

I am asking your assistance in having all of the old account numbers deleted from my credit report and reference the most recent, which is 05-123456789. I spoke with (Name of contact) from this office and he advised me that the prefix of these account numbers are loan office locations, but the reports read as if I have five separate account numbers and it lowers my score.

Please have the old account numbers referenced on my credit report deleted and reference the latest account number of 05-123456789.

I look forward to your reply and working with (Name of creditor) to become a better client.

Sincerely,

Signature

(Your typed full legal name)

Unauthorized Inquiries

Date

Your Address

Creditor
Address
City, State Zip Code

ATTN: Credit Reporting Department

RE: Credit Report - Unauthorized Credit Inquiry (Date of inquiry referenced on credit report) for SSN (Insert your social security number)

Dear Creditor:

I recently received a copy of my credit report from (credit bureau), and I may be a victim of identity theft. The credit report showed a credit inquiry by your company that I do not recall authorizing. I understand that creditors should not be allowed to put an inquiry on my file unless I have authorized it. The signature authorizing it should match that of the one provided below.

Please have this inquiry removed from my credit file because it is making it very difficult for me to acquire credit.

Please also forward to me, written confirmation of the removal of this unauthorized inquiry.

If you find that I am remiss, and you did have my authorization to inquire into my credit report, please send me proof of this.

Thanking you in advance,

Signature

(Your typed full legal name)

Corporate Account on Personal Records

Date

Your Address

Collection Agency for Corporate Account
Address
City, State Zip Code

RE: Corporate Account Creditor - Account number (Insert account number) on submitted dispute file number (Reference number from on-line credit dispute with credit bureau) dated (Date)

Dear (Collection agency contact):

It was a pleasure speaking with you on (Date of contact) regarding the dilemma I am having with the inappropriate corporate account posting with (Corporate account creditor) on my personal credit report.

As we discussed, this was originally a corporate account with (Corporate account creditor) for a company I previously owned (Name of your company). This company was incorporated in the state of (State) as an (Type of corporation e.g., "S" Corporation) and held a corporate checking account with (Name of bank in City, State). Its tax ID numbers can be cross-referenced with the Internal Revenue Service as (Tax ID number/FEIN). The addresses for (Name of your company) was:

Company address
City, State, Zip Code

Feel free to contact me for any additional questions regarding this matter at the address above or via telephone at (Your current telephone number).

Sincerely,

Signature

(Your typed full legal name)

Address Reference

Date

Your Address

Credit Bureau
Address
City, State Zip Code

ATTN: Dispute Resolution

RE: Personal Information - Name, address and consumer statement for Confirmation number (Number received from online credit report)

Dear (Name of credit bureau):

My correct name is (Your full legal name).

My correct address is:

(Most recent address)

Please delete all other names, addresses and existing consumer statement from my credit report.

I look forward to a prompt reply as confirmation that my account has been properly corrected.

Sincerely,

Signature

(Your typed full legal name)

Enclosed: Copy of driver license

Present and Previous Employer

Date

Your Address

Credit Bureau
Address
City, State Zip Code

ATTN: Dispute Resolution

RE: Personal Information - Present and Previous Employers for Confirmation number (Number received from online credit report)

Dear (Name of credit bureau):

Please delete all other employment references on my credit report and replace with the following:

Present Employer:

Employer Name: AUTOZONE, INC.
Position: DISTRIBUTION CENTER MGR.
Location: PHOENIX, AZ
Hired: 06/2002

Previous Employer:

Employer Name: JIFFY LUBE INTL., INC.
Position: SERVICE CENTER MGR.
Location: HOUSTON, TX
Hired: 07/1997

Employer Name: CSK AUTO, INC.
Position: ASSISTANT MANAGER
Location: HOBBS, NM
Hired: 01/1992

I look forward to receiving my revised credit report.

Sincerely,

Signature

(Your typed full legal name)

ABC's of Credit Terminology

The following terms will assist you in interpreting credit related documents and effectively communicating with financial institutions, credit bureaus and collection agencies.

A

Account
A formal banking or business relationship established to provide for regular services and other financial transactions.

Account Number
A unique, consumer assigned and owned alpha-numeric account reference number, assigned by the creditor or collection agency.

Adverse Action
Action taken by a creditor or other entity negatively affecting a consumer the consumer.

Adverse Information
Information about a consumer that a creditor or other entity referencing the consumer as a risk or unacceptable.

Annual Percentage Rate (APR)
The periodic rate times the number of periods in a year.

B

Bankruptcy
A law for a debtor that, upon voluntary petition or one invoked by the debtor's creditors, is judged legally insolvent. The debtor's remaining property is then administered for the creditors or is distributed among them.

C

Chapter 7 Bankruptcy
A bankruptcy option in which a bankrupt firm is liquidated after the courts have determined that reorganization is not worthwhile. A trustee is charged with liquidating all assets and distributing the proceeds to satisfy claims in their order of priority. In Chapter 7 bankruptcies the creditors often receive a fraction of the value of their claims and the stockholders receive nothing.

Chapter 11 Bankruptcy
A bankruptcy option in which a trustee is appointed to reorganize the bankrupt firm. Although the existing claims of security holders are likely to be reduced or replaced with different claims, it is expected that the firm will continue operating. Both creditors and owners must vote approval of the plan before the reorganization can be confirmed by court action and become effective.

Chapter 13 Bankruptcy
A bankruptcy option in which debtors repay debts according to a plan accepted by the debtor, the creditors, and the court.

Charge card
A credit card that must be paid in full at the end of the month.

Charge card check digit
A security measure for paying through the Internet. These digits are only printed on the credit card.

Credit
A consumer's ability to make purchases, obtain services, or borrow money based on his or her promise, ability, and demonstrated willingness to repay.

Credit bureau
An agency that collects, researches and manages consumer history and in turn provides that information to potential creditors, employers and others who have permission to inquire about the creditworthiness of that consumer.

Credit card
A financially limited card which allows a consumer to pay a portion or all of the outstanding amount each month.

Credit check
The formal inquiry to confirm a consumer's credit payment history.

Credit history
The record of a consumer's past borrowing and repaying behavior over a certain duration of time.

Credit limit
The maximum balance that can be carried on a credit account.

Credit insurance
The insurance on a loan and protection of income and debt is paid in case the consumer becomes disabled, loses a job or dies.

Credit report
The credit bureau's summary of a consumer's credit history over a duration of time.

Credit risk
The assessment of a consumer's likelihood of fulfilling the terms of a credit agreement.

Credit scoring
The statistical technique that combines financial characteristics to form a single score to represent a consumer's creditworthiness.

Creditor
A lender of money.

Creditworthy
Having an acceptable credit rating.

D

Date closed
The date when a credit agreement or account was terminated.

Date opened
The date when a credit account was established.

Default
Failure to pay money when it is due.

Deferment
The postponement of payment until a later time.

Direct deposit
The deposit of funds directly into a bank account as a form of payment.

Dispute
The disagreement about the accuracy of information in a credit report.

F

Fair Credit Reporting Act (FCRA)
Provides consumers with the right to obtain copies of their credit reports for free if denied credit; defines obsolete information; and declares that reasonable procedures must be used to ensure accuracy.

Finance charge
The additional fees one pays to pay for a retail item in installments.

Forbearance
The act of a creditor who refrains from enforcing a debt when it falls due.

Fraud
The deliberate practicing of deception to secure unfair or unlawful gain.

G

Grace period
The period of time before the borrower must begin or resume repaying a loan or debt.

I

Identity
The distinct personality of an individual regarded as a persisting entity; individuality. Also includes driver's license, social security number and date of birth.

Identity theft
The crime of stealing credit card numbers, college degrees, addresses, social security numbers, etc., for illegal use.

Installment loan
A loan with equal and fixed payment amounts.

Installment loan account number
A unique, consumer assigned and owned alpha-numeric account reference number, assigned by the creditor to a specific installment loan account

Interest
A charge for a loan, usually a percentage of the amount loaned.

Interest rate
The percentage of a sum of money charged for its use.

L

Lien
The legal right or interest that a creditor has in another property that last until the obligation is paid or satisfied.

Line of credit
The informal loan arrangement between a bank and a customer allowing the customer to borrow up to a pre-specified amount.

M

Mortgage
A loan secured by the collateral of some specified real estate property that obliges the borrower to make a predetermined series of payments.

Mortgage account number
The unique, consumer assigned and owned alpha-numeric account reference number, assigned by the creditor that can be found on the monthly mortgage statement.

O

Open account
An account that is active, still in use, or is still being paid.

Open end lease
A lease agreement that provides for an additional payment at the expiration of the lease to adjust for any change in the value of the property.

P

Paid as agreed
The credit report designation indicating the consumer is repaying or has paid the credit according to the terms of the credit agreement.

Periodic rate
The most effective interest rate.

Promotional inquiry
The inquiry made into a consumer's credit report for purposes of a promotional offer.

Public records
A record filed in a public office.

R

Refinance
The extension and/or increase in amount of existing debt.

Repossession
To reclaim possession of property by a creditor.

Retail credit
The credit granted to a consumer for the purchase of goods or services.

Revolving charge account
The credit automatically available up to a pre-determined limit so long as a consumer makes regular payments.

S

Settlement
The resolution of a dispute or payment made.

W

Wire transfer
The electronic transfer of funds.

References

Hartwig, R.P. & Wilkinson, C. (June 2003). The Use of Credit Information in Personal Lines Insurance Underwriting (Insurance Information Institute, Insurance Issues Series, Vol. 1, No. 2). Retrieved June 2005, from www.iii.org

Insurance Information Institute. Credit Scoring. (May 2005). Retrieved June 2005, from www.iii.org

About the Author

Alton lives in Phoenix, Arizona. He received his A.A. degree from New Mexico Military Institute, his B.S. in Aviation Business Administration from Embry-Riddle Aeronautical University, and M.S. in Management Science from the University of Central Texas.

His interests include writing, public speaking, singing, and aviation. He also pursues acting in independent film, as well as local and national commercials.